The Bath

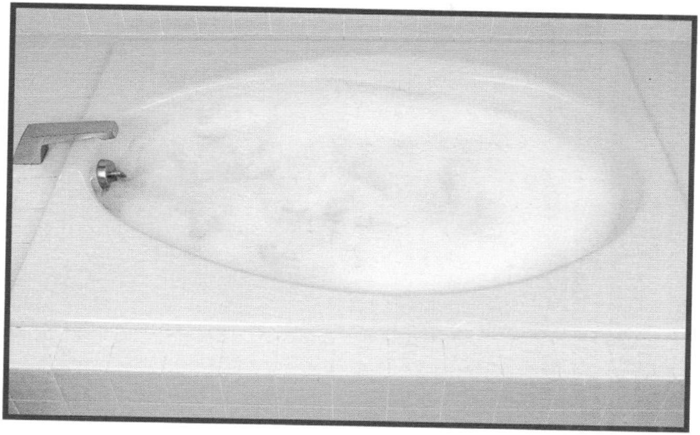

Written by Judy Nayer
Photographs by Michael Gaffney

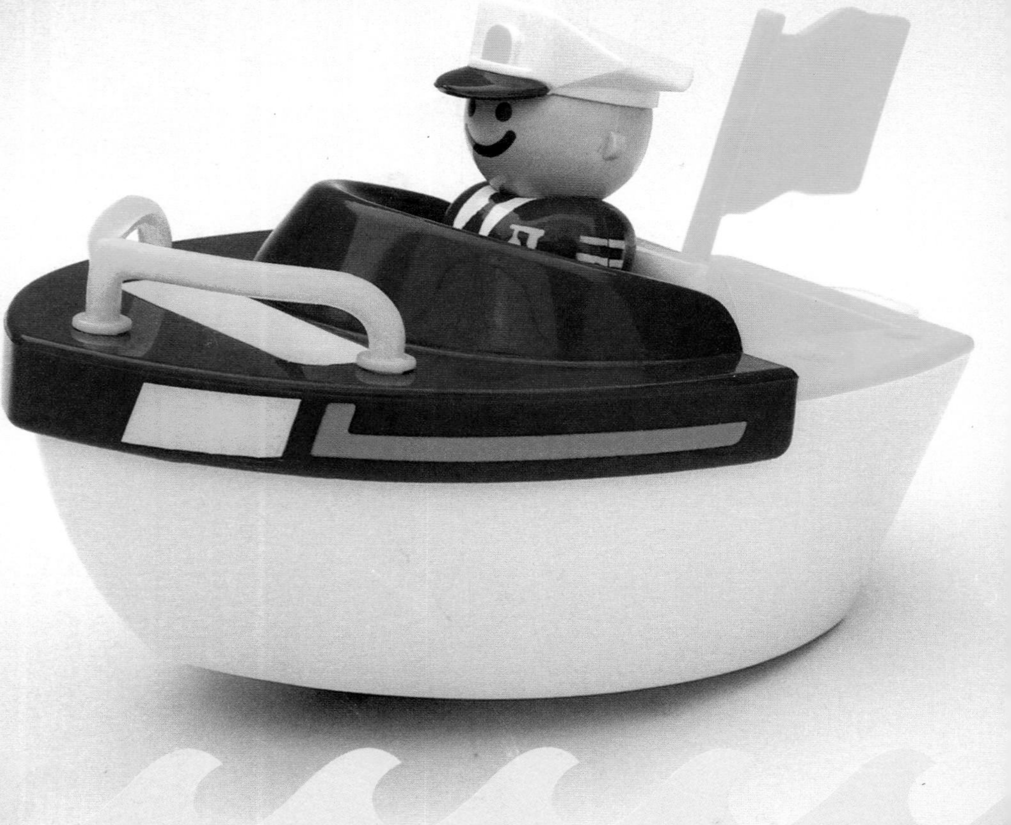

A boat,

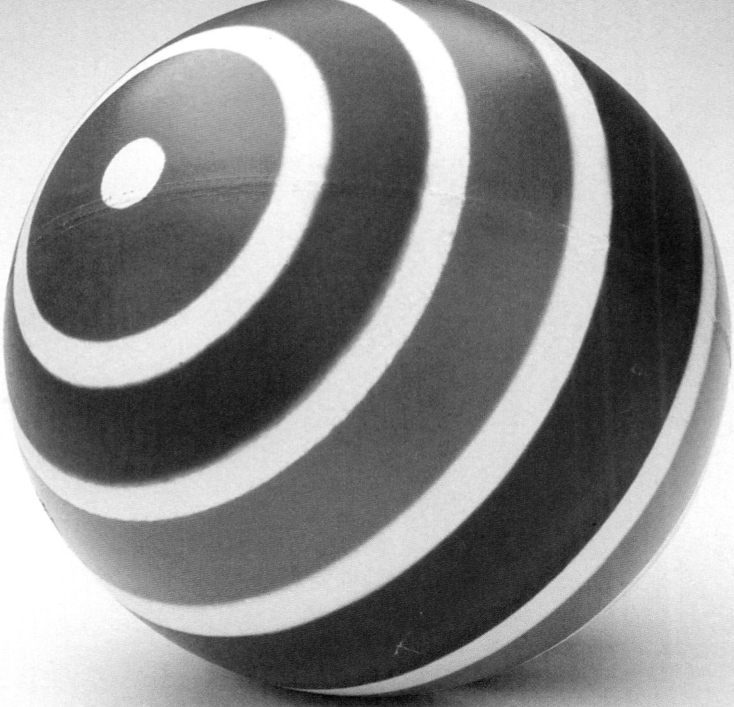

a ball,

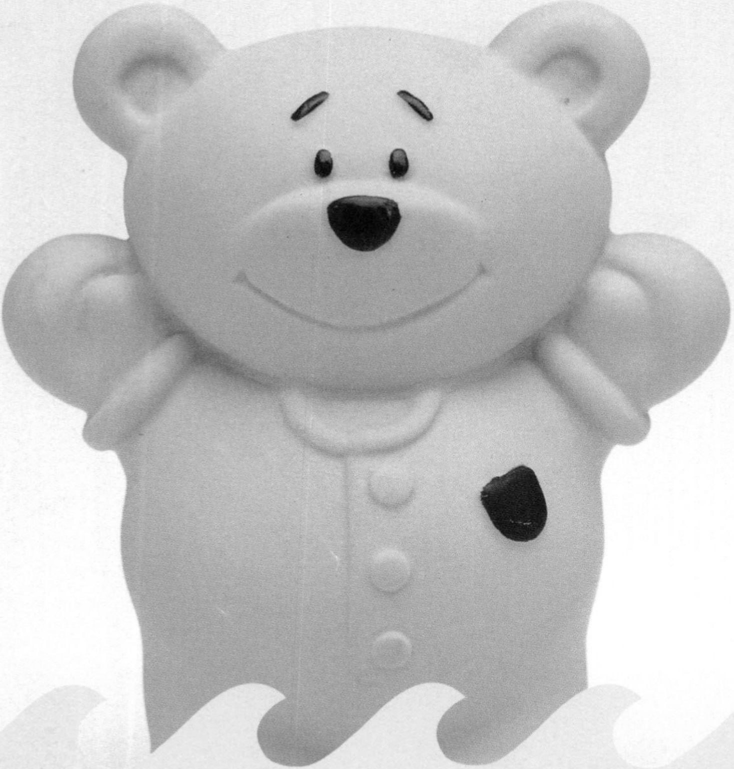

a bear,

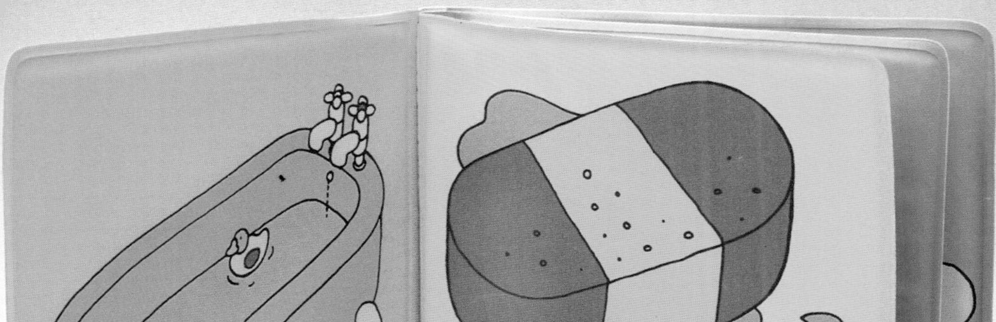

a book,

a bubble,

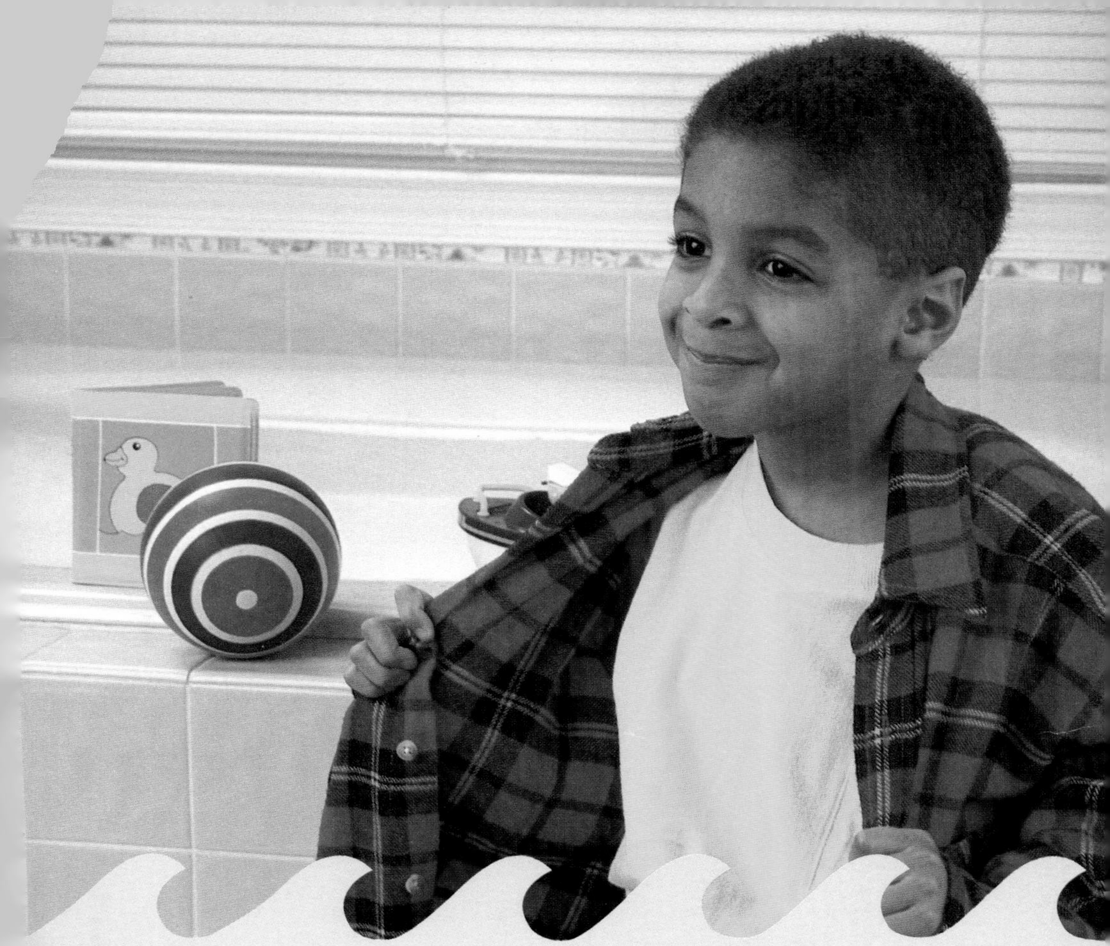

a boy,

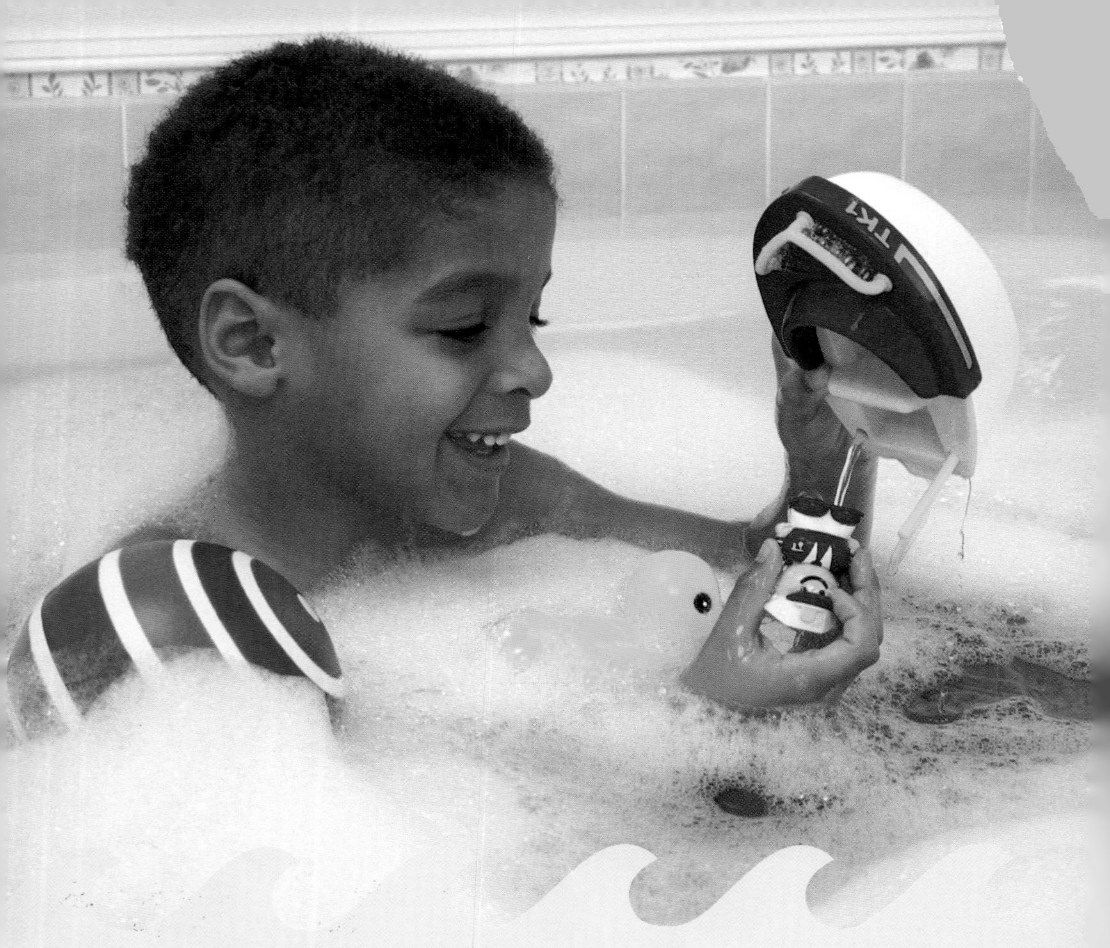

a bath!